Beginner's Meditation Guide for the Busy Mind

Learn to meditate from scratch and on the go

Introduction

I want to thank you and congratulate you for downloading the book, "Meditation: Beginner's Meditation Guide for the Busy Mind -- Learn to Meditate from Scratch and On the Go."

This book contains proven steps and strategies on how to develop a useful, convenient, and sensible practice of meditation that will fit into your busy lifestyle. It provides insights and practical tips to help you start your practice even if you lead a hectic, demanding, and stressful life.

Using the recommendations outlined in this book, you will be able to concentrate better and work more productively. You will acquire better focus, feel less anxious about things, become calmer and more peaceful, connect with your thoughts and feelings, and understand yourself better. Your life may still be the same, but you will be more accepting, more appreciative, and happier.

Thanks again for purchasing this book, I hope you enjoy it!

Chapter 1: What is Meditation?

The word meditation comes from two Latin words: meditari (to train the mind, to think, to focus) and mederi (to cure or to heal). It is derived from the Sanskrit word "medha" which means wisdom.

When you meditate, you try to quiet the mind and gain focus. As you grow in the practice of meditation, you eventually reach a high level of inner calm and awareness.

In the past, people thought that meditation was only for "special" people like ancient mystics, Buddhist monks, yogis, priests, and the like. People believed that you had to be in a temple, burn incense, engage in certain rituals, and don the proper attire in order to practice meditation.

Today, people understand that meditation is for everyone. You can meditate at any time and basically anywhere. While some people feel that certain elements like clothes and incense may help deepen the practice, these elements are not really essential. They may even distract others from achieving focus.

Today, a growing number of people want to achieve a sense of peace and tranquillity through meditation. Meditation has crossed the threshold and entered the mainstream.

The practice of meditation is associated with a lot of positive things. People meditate for different reasons. Some individuals practice it for health and wellness, while others want to achieve growth and aspire for enlightenment.

For many, meditation has become a way of life. It has become possible even for busy people to practice meditation. Even if you think you have limited time, you can still do meditation. You simply have to focus and turn your attention inwards. Regardless of what is happening around you, you can silence your mind, free your mind from scattered thoughts, focus your attention on one object, and achieve a clear and relaxed inner state.

In today's busy world, you can watch your breath, listen to the birds, go walking and just focus on your breath. When you are able to free your mind from all other distracting elements, you are doing meditation.

Chapter 2: What are the Benefits of Meditation?

With meditation, your body goes through positive changes. You will notice that you have more energy (prana). With the constant practice of meditation, the level of prana in your body increases thereby enhancing your body, mind, and spirit.

Meditation can result in the following physical benefits:

- Reduced blood pressure

- Reduced levels of blood lactate resulting in reduced levels of anxiety and stress

- Fewer stress-related pain like ulcers, tension headaches, insomnia, and joint and muscle pains

- Higher levels of serotonin, resulting in better moods

- Stronger immune system

- Higher energy level

- Slower aging

- Improved sense of general well-being

Meditation results in relaxed brain patterns that promote healing. When you practice meditation regularly, you achieve the following results:

- Reduced anxiety

- Greater emotional stability

- Increased creativity

- Stronger intuition

- Peace of mind

- Clarity of thoughts

- Improved concentration

- Increased joy and enthusiasm

- Calmer disposition

- Sharper mind

- Fewer feelings of frustration, tension, and anger

- Greater self-knowledge and appreciation

- Improved relationships

- Personal transformation

You need to practice meditation regularly so you will experience its many benefits. If you are a beginner, it is prudent to learn about things essential to the practice of meditation.

Chapter 3: The Basics of Meditation

Preparing to Meditate

- Choose a nice, quiet place.

Choose a place that is relatively quiet and calm. Such an environment will help you focus on what you are about to do. Choose somewhere private and peaceful. If possible, limit all types of distractions. Turn off the phone and the television set. If you prefer to meditate with music, make sure that you choose something mild, gently rhythmic, and calming. You can also opt to listen to the sound of running water from a miniature water fountain.

The place does not have to be absolutely silent. It is alright to hear the neighbor's dog barking or the washing machine running. Everyday sounds should not keep you from meditating effectively. You can meditate and be aware of the noise around you. You should, however, learn not to allow such noise to dominate your thoughts.

You can also opt to meditate outdoors. You can choose a cool shady spot in your garden or sit under a tree.

- Use comfortable clothes.

You want to meditate so you can still your mind and block off external noise. You will find this difficult to do if you are wearing tight, uncomfortable clothes. It is better to wear loose clothing that allows you to breathe comfortably.

Use a cardigan if the place is cool. Otherwise, you will be constantly thinking about how cold it is and end your practice too soon. If you are taking some time off from work to meditate – and can't change your clothes, just make sure that you are as comfortable as you can be. Take off your belt, unbutton your collar, remove your shoes, and take off your jacket.

- Decide on a time frame.

How long do you want to meditate? People who have been practicing meditation for quite some time now usually do two 20-minute sessions every day. If you are a beginner, you can opt to start out with a daily 5-minute session and progress from there.

It is better to set a regular schedule – and try to stick to it. You can do it first thing in the morning, at lunch, or before bedtime. Try to make this schedule a regular part of your everyday routine.

Do not expect to see immediate results though. You need time and constant practice before you enjoy the benefits. Try to enjoy the process.

- Do some light stretches prior to meditation.

You will have to sit still in one spot while meditating. As you advance in your practice, you may want to meditate in the lotus position. It will help you meditate more effectively if you prepare for it by doing some light stretches before you start meditating. Loosen up the muscles in your neck, shoulders, lower back, thighs, and legs to prevent tension or pain while meditating. If you do not take the time to stretch out these muscles, you may experience some pain while meditating and lose your concentration.

How to Meditate

- Posture

By tradition, people who meditate assume the half-lotus or the lotus position for their practice. They sit on the ground or on a cushion. The posture requires a certain degree of flexibility, particularly of the back, hips, thighs, and legs. Otherwise, your lower back will bow and you will have a tough time keeping your torso balanced.

It is essential to feel comfortable while you meditate. If you lack the flexibility for the traditional posture, find a position that is comfortable for you. You can opt not to cross your legs, but you need to tilt your pelvis frontwards so you can center your spine squarely over the two bones on your butt that carry your weight. A meditation bench usually has a tilted seat. If your seat is not tilted, just put something underneath it that will serve to incline it forward by about half an inch or so. Alternatively, you can use a thick cushion and sit on the front edge.

It is imperative that you are relaxed and comfortable. Balance your torso so that your spine is able to shore up the entire weight of your upper body, neck, and head. If you feel any strain, take the time to loosen up the area without slumping. Always check your posture and realign your torso if necessary.

The traditional posture requires that you rest your hands on your lap. The palms face upward, with the left hand underneath the right. You can also opt to simply put your hands on your knees or have them hang on your sides. Do whatever feels right for you.

Some people meditate with their eyes closed. Others opt to keep their eyes open. If you are a beginner, it may be more prudent to close your eyes during your first few tries. This will help contain visual distractions and help you focus on keeping your mind still.

When you have become more familiar with the practice of meditation, you can try to meditate with open eyes. Some people find that keeping their eyes open helps keep them awake. Keep your eyes "soft." Do not focus them on any object in particular. Your objective is to remain calm but awake. Do not try to go into a trance.

- Breathing

Breathing is basic to the practice of meditation. One of the most basic forms of meditation simply requires you to sit in a cross-legged position, to keep your back straight, and focus on your breathing.

Focus on your inhalation and exhalation. Choose a spot directly on top of your navel and center your mind on that. Pay attention to your abdomen as it rises and falls with your breathing. Breathe normally. You do not have to exert any effort to modify your breathing pattern.

Focus your mind on your breathing by becoming aware of it.

You may choose to have a mental image to help you with this exercise. You can think of a coin lying on that spot over your navel and see it rise and fall as you breathe in and breathe out. You can think of a buoy floating on the sea and see it bob up and down as you inhale and exhale. Or, you can think of a lotus flower sitting on your belly and watch it unfurl its petals as your breathing swells and lulls.

Your mind may wander during this exercise, but there is nothing to worry about. This is normal, particularly if you are a beginner. Just bring your mind back to your breathing. Keep your mind empty except for the breathing.

- Counting

You can do this meditation exercise with your eyes closed. Make sure that you are sitting up straight with your torso resting squarely on your butt. Count ONE silently while breathing in deeply through your nose. Then, slowly expel the breath, also through your nose, while you silently count TWO.

Do this repeatedly until you reach TEN.

It is not unlikely for your mind to drift or for you to lose count. Do not lose patience. Simply start over.

Chapter 4: Is Meditation for Busy People?

People who meditate say that they are better people because of this practice. Even if you believe them, you may think you do not have the time for meditation. You simply are TOO Busy! You have a million things on your plate! You do not have enough time and your mind is constantly racing. How can you find the time, let alone the energy and wherewithal, to clear it? You think you do not have what it takes to sit still and calm your mind. You have a long list of important tasks that you have to accomplish and you simply cannot afford to just sit down and meditate.

Your hesitation and doubts are usually grounded in the belief that when you agree to practice meditation, you have to do it right from the get go. You think that your meditation has to be perfect, or at the very least, easy and smooth right from the beginning. It DOES NOT have to be.

Meditation is like everything else in life. You just have to show up and be there. You create a practice that is right and comfortable for you. It does not have to be perfect. You can work on it and improve it little by little.

What keeps a lot of people from attempting meditation is the thought that they have to follow a lot of rules. They think that meditation is a rigid practice. This is not true.

Meditate means to reflect or contemplate. It is a way to connect with your true self. It is not limited to sitting absolutely still in a faultless lotus position with hands in Surya Mudra, Buddhi Mudra or any of the Mudra positions. You can meditate in many ways.

Even if you are short on time or are always busy, you can go on short proactive meditations and get the full benefits of the meditation practice. You do not even have to sit still to do it. You can meditate on the go.

You can meditate while walking on a busy city street or on a country road. You can meditate while on your way to the office on a bus. You can meditate on an airplane on your way to an out-of-town conference. You can meditate while in the shower. You can meditate in your office during lunch break. Even if you are "wildly" busy, you can find a few minutes to meditate. In fact, you SHOULD cultivate the practice of meditation especially if you lead a strongly demanding and hectic life.

Is your mind constantly swirling with thoughts and worries? Are you always thinking about the important presentations you have to make, the challenging negotiation you have to work out, or the difficult conversation you have to initiate? Are you always in a state of anxiety, thinking and worrying about what is going to happen next? Are you always planning for the future? Do you feel that you are missing out on life? If you are, then you are likely to benefit from meditation for busy people.

You do not have to push yourself or struggle to meditate "properly." You can experience the benefits of meditation even if you do not spend 30 minutes a day in meditative bliss sitting with your spine perfectly upright.

Many simple acts can be a form of meditation. What is essential is that you try to keep your mind focused on the here and now.

Chapter 5: Meditations on the Go for the Busy Mind

You can incorporate the practice of meditation into your busy daily routine. There are several forms of meditation that you can do.

· *Walking Meditation*

You can do a walking meditation. It is an alternative form of meditation that allows you to notice how your feet move and how your body connects to the earth. If you intend to go on a protracted seated meditation, it may be beneficial to break up the session a couple of times with a walking meditation.

Select a quiet spot with a minimum of distractions. You do not need a large area. Choose a place where it will allow you to take seven straight paces before you have to turn back. It is also good to do a walking meditation barefoot, if possible.

Turn your gaze straight ahead. Hold your head up. Clasp your hands firmly but gently in front of you. Using your right foot, make a slow, measured step forward. Focus on the movement. Stop for a few seconds after the first step. Step with the left foot, concentrating on the movement. Then stop once again. Make sure that each step is slow and deliberate. Move one foot at a time.

Upon reaching the end of the pathway, stop moving completely. Keep the feet together. Make a slow turn. Walk back to where you first started. Make sure that you use the same unhurried and deliberate motions.

When you do the walking meditation, you focus on how your feet move in the same manner that you focus on your breathing when you do the breathing meditation. Clear your mind of everything. Concentrate on how your foot connects to the earth.

· *Meditation While Taking the Bus or Subway, a Train, or a Plane*

Most people simply listen to music on their cell phones, read the newspaper, or just plain zone out when they take the bus or subway to or from work. There is nothing wrong with this. However, you can use your commute time to meditate. You can use the time to foster inner peace. If you are a busy person, you can carve out this space to meditate and clear your mind.

You can meditate while standing or sitting. If it is safe to do so, you may close your eyes. Or you can choose one thing to focus on; make sure that your gaze remains soft and relaxed.

Go through the different parts of your body. Go slowly from head to toe. If a part seems taut or uncomfortable, make a conscious effort to let go of the tightness.

Bring your awareness to your surroundings. What sounds do you notice? How is the temperature? Is it warm or cool?

These initial steps are intended to make you aware of the present moment.

Next, focus your mind on your breathing. Observe the subtleties of your breathing. Are you breathing fast or slow? Is your breathing deep or shallow? The objective is to gain awareness – not to judge whether or not you are breathing the right way.

You can increase the awareness of your breathing by counting one as you inhale and two as you exhale. You shouldn't feel frustrated if your attention wanders. This is completely normal. It may even occur repeatedly. Just direct your wandering mind back to counting your breaths.

There are many things that may cause your mind to drift from the breath. You may think certain thoughts, remember things you have to do, or become distracted by the problems you have to solve. You may become distracted by other commuters. You may be sidetracked by the noisy clank of the bus' engine. You may feel bored, frustrated, or anxious. Notice what has distracted you ("I am feeling bored") and then gently direct your focus back to your breathing.

Sometimes, you may find it tough to block out significantly noticeable movements or loud noises. Just keep in mind that the goal is not to tune them out completely. The goal is to center your attention on your breathing even if there are distractions.

This meditation practice may seem quite simple. It may look passive, requiring minimal effort. It really is not that easy, especially if you are just a beginner.

You may become discouraged when your mind refuses to stay put and continues to wander. Bear in mind that wandering is to be expected. The real goal is to continue to gently bring your focus back to the present moment. The mind will stray.

However, if you continue to return to the breath again and again, you will be able to enjoy the benefits of the process.

You can meditate for 5 or 10 minutes while on the bus or subway. Keep watch of the time by setting a timer on your watch or phone.

You can also do this kind of meditation while taking a train or an airplane.

There are many other forms of meditation that you can do on the go. They are a special boon for busy people who can't find the time to go on guided meditations with a mentor.

· *Meditating with your Pet*

You probably spend some time with your pet, petting and bonding with him. You can combine meditation with showing affection for your pet dog or pet cat. By doing the exercise in a consciously mindful manner, petting your pet can become a meditation experience.

Keep your mind on what you are doing. Focus on your breathing. Focus on how it feels when you are petting your dog. Your touch will calm and comfort your dog. At the same time, you will feel relaxed. The exercise will lower your heart rate. It will release endorphins, the feel-good or happy hormones, and results in a calmer, happier you.

If you do not have a dog or cat to pet, you can watch fish in an aquarium. Focusing your mind on what you see and on your breathing will help reduce tension and alleviate anxiety.

· *Meditating While Driving*

Before you consider this form of meditation, make sure that you consider your safety first.

People who drive usually find themselves tuning things out and getting lost in thought. However, they get to where they want to go safely.

You, too, probably have experienced driving to your destination and wondering, at the back of your mind, how you got there. You, too, probably got lost in thought. You

13

can become so conditioned to doing something habitually that you do it routinely, without paying due attention to what you are doing. This takes you out of the present moment.

Meditating while driving keeps you engaged in the experience. You focus on the driving experience, on the here and now.

When you drive to and from a certain destination, you are in transition. You may lean towards the future and think about the friends you are going to see after work. You may lean towards the past and can't seem to be able to truly "leave" work. You continue to think about the day's events and problems. As you drive, you are either anticipating the future or staying trapped in the past.

Meditating while driving gives you the opportunity to become mindful of the present moment.

It is important to bear in mind that reaching your destination safely is of primary importance. If you are a beginner in meditation, it is best that you start your meditation practice at home or somewhere quiet with few distractions. Once you feel more comfortable in the practice and know exactly how you respond to meditation, you may try meditation while driving.

Many forms of meditation focus on the breath. Meditation while driving focuses on what you are doing in the here and now – which is driving. You focus your mind on the elements fundamental to driving a vehicle – the motions you go through, as well as the use of vision, hearing, and your other senses.

You can meditate while driving for about 5 minutes at one time. Make sure that you take a break. You may opt to do another 5 minutes of meditation after the break. Once you enjoy the benefits that come with the practice of meditation, you may want to spend your commute meditating in 5-minute sessions with breaks in between.

Turn off your car radio. Become aware of how it feels to be inside the car.

Focus your mind on the physical "feel" of driving. Become aware of your hands as they rest on the steering wheel. Become aware of your body as you sit on the car seat. Notice how the pedals feel under your feet.

Focus your mind on other physical sensations. Do your shoulders feel tense? Is your back hunched? Consciously tell your body to release all the tension it feels.

Pay attention to your surroundings. Become aware of the sounds that you hear. Take note of the road and its characteristics. Notice what the cars around you look like.

Create meditation rituals. Every time you have to stop at a crosswalk, a stop light or a stop sign, pause and breathe deeply.

Each time your mind wanders – as it is bound to – just bring your focus back to the elements already mentioned. Your mind is likely to drift in what seasoned meditation practitioners refer to as "monkey mind." Notice when your mind drifts off, and gently coach it back to the present moment. Don't fuss about how tough – or easy, it is for you to be present in the moment.

· *Loving-Kindness Meditation*

The loving-kindness meditation focuses on trying to evoke vast and intense feelings of loving kindness toward the self and other people.

Sit in a relaxed and comfortable position. Take deep long breaths, exhaling slowly after you inhale. Let go of all your concerns. Focus on each breath as it moves through the middle of your chest – around the area where your heart is.

As you sit quietly, mentally send loving-kindness thoughts to yourself. Repeat the phrases over and over, making sure that you say them in slow, steady, and deliberate measures.

"May I be peaceful." "May I be joyful." "May I be content." "May I be well." "May I be at ease."

As you think of these thoughts, connect to the intentions of wishing yourself loving happiness. If you start to have feelings of kindness, warmth, openness, or love, try to connect with them, nurturing them as you continue to mentally repeat the phrases.

You can reinforce the intentions you are expressing by embracing a mental image of yourself. The genial feelings you have are likely to grow stronger as you continue with the repetitions.

After some time, you can start to direct loving-kindness toward a friend or a loved one. Do the same thing -- this time directing your thoughts toward this friend.

"May you be peaceful." "May you be joyful." "May you be content." "May you be well." "May you be at ease."

As you send the loving-kindness thoughts, connect to their meaning and heartfelt intention. If you start to have feelings of kindness and love, connect to the feelings. The feelings are likely to grow more intense as you continue repeating the words.

Proceed with the meditation. This time, you can think about a neighbor, another friend, an acquaintance, a stranger, your pet, and finally individuals whom you have hurt or who have hurt you.

You can repeat the same phrases, saying them over and over again. You can also formulate phrases that better embody your loving-kindness intentions and feelings towards the person you have in your mind.

You may feel conflicting emotions of sorrow, grief, resentment, or anger as you go through your meditation. Take these feelings to reveal what you hold in your heart. Take these feelings to signify that your heart is starting to soften. Accept the feelings with grace and patience. You can modify your meditation to a breathing meditation if the negative feelings persist. Accept the negative feelings as real. Let them be. Or you can go on with the loving-kindness meditation, mustering as much acceptance and kindness as possible.

Allow feelings of acceptance to prevail. Do not be judgmental – of yourself or of the person you are thinking of.

·   *Other Simple Ways to Incorporate the Spirit of Meditation into Your Day to Day Routine*

Simply be aware. Try to stop thinking, labeling, or judging what you are doing. Maintain an open and accepting attitude.

During your meditation, you will not be able to stay in the present moment all the time. When your thoughts wander, focus on your breathing. Feeling and hearing yourself breathe in and breathe out mindfully will help check your wandering thoughts and get your attention back to the moment.

There will be times when you will experience nagging thoughts. You may have issues, problems, ideas, or nagging to-dos that crop up and refuse to go away. Try to focus on these thoughts. Imagine that you are putting each thought on a leaf and watching the leaf drift away on a stream. As another thought comes up, imagine the same thing. As you put a thought on a leaf and watch it drift off, focus on your breathing.

Accept your meditation experience for what it is. Do not analyze it or be critical about it. Do not fret about how you are doing. Do not be anxious about making progress. Just try to keep a calm mind. Focus on the present moment and accept it for being what it is.

Your meditation may not conform to the perfect image of the ideal solitary practice of meditation. If it works for you – if it gets you focused on the present moment and calms you, then you are in a good place.

Chapter 6: Things to Consider When Meditating in Public

You can go on different forms of meditation in public. You can meditate on a train, in the bus, on an airplane, or in a park. Meditating in public allows you to squeeze in time for your practice. If you equate meditation with being alone in a quiet room with nothing to distract you, you curtail your opportunities to meditate, especially if you are busy with work, family, and other obligations. If you do not mind meditating "on the go," you lay yourself open to limitless occasions for meditation.

However, there are some things you have to keep in mind when you meditate in public.

- Do not expect to find it as easy to focus on your breathing.

You are likely to become frustrated. It is better to cultivate awareness about the sights, smells, and sounds around you as part of the exercise. Focus on the light, sound, and space. Acknowledge their presence, no matter how unpleasant. Allow their unrestrained passage through your mind. If you do this, sometimes, you will find that they are no longer the distractions they once were. You may find yourself better able to focus on other things – your breathing for example, even if you are still aware of the elements of your surroundings.

- Meditating in public carries with it the risk of being interrupted.

You may be approached by people curious about what you are doing. Do not become annoyed by the interruption. Let it be. You are not in a special room exclusively dedicated to the practice of meditation. You do not have a "do not disturb" sign hanging near you. You are in a public place. Deal with the interruption with as much grace as you can.

- If you are meditating on the bus, train, or park, you may want to consider doing it while seated in a normal manner with your hands on your lap.

Keeping your hands in the ritual or symbolic meditation mudra position may provoke attention, which you may not welcome.

Many individuals associate meditation with going up the mountain or hiding deep in the forest to seek silence and seclusion. It is interesting to note that many people think that Buddha may have meditated while walking in relatively accessible "normal "public places.

Buddha was believed to beg and walk close to town – and may have done so while meditating. Meditating this way – in public and visible to other people -- has the effect of making the practice of meditation seem ordinary and available to all. If more people engage in the practice even while living very busy in their lives, more people will be able to enjoy the many benefits that come with the regular practice of meditation.

Chapter 7: More Tips for Beginners

The following are tips that many individuals find useful when they are just starting their practice. They will help you get started, and they will help you sustain your practice. You do not have to try everything all at the same time. Start small; start easy. And, the most important of all, enjoy the benefits that come with the practice.

- Sit still for just a couple of minutes.

Does this sound so easy that it seems almost ridiculous? That's just fine. Set aside two minutes a day to meditate. Do this for a week. After a week, if you feel that two minutes is not enough, increase the time. Increase the duration a little at a time as you deem suitable. Before you know it, you will be meditating 15 minutes a day – or even more, and finding the exercise gratifying. Make sure that you start small.

- Meditate first thing in the morning.

It is easy to convince yourself that you are going to meditate every day. However, your daily routine will soon catch up with you and you will find it difficult to find the time. Do it every morning – and set the right tone for your day.

- Don't fuss about how you are going to do it. Just do it.

If you fret about where to meditate, how to sit, and all the details, you will find it too tiresome to begin. So get seated – on the chair, on your bed, on the couch, or on the floor – it does not really matter where as long as you are comfortable. Just sit; it will only be for two minutes anyway. As you progress with your practice, you will be able to find means to optimize your time. But as a beginner, just do it.

- Do not agonize over whether you are doing it the right way.

There is no absolute right way. As long as you are comfortable and at ease, you are doing fine.

- Be aware of how you feel.

Do you feel any tension in your body? Where do you feel the tightness? Try to ease the tension where you feel it. Are you bored, uncomfortable, or anxious? Accept your feelings without judgment. It is completely okay to have these feelings.

- Focus on your breathing.

Try to settle down by concentrating on your breath. Focus on it as you inhale deeply. Follow your breath as it goes through your nose and fills your chest. Focus on it as you exhale and let it out of your chest and out of your nose. Count "one" as you breathe in slowly and "two" as you breathe out. Count all the way to ten. Then repeat the process from "one."

- Accept the fact that your mind will wander.

There is nothing wrong with this. Do not feel frustrated. If you cannot stay focused, that is perfectly fine. Simply start over. Gently nudge your thoughts back to counting your breaths.

- Nurture a loving disposition.

When thoughts and feeling arise while you are meditating, look upon them with an accepting attitude. Do not view them as adversaries or intruders. Although they do not represent you, they are an intrinsic part of you. Do not be harsh or judgmental -- even with yourself.

- Do not fret about not being able to absolutely "clear your mind."

Meditation is not about keeping the mind empty or clearing it of all thoughts. This may occur at times but it is not the primary purpose for meditating. Just try to focus your attention – and gently nudge your mind back when it drifts.

- Accept your feelings.

Sometimes, you may have thoughts and feelings that you initially think as contrary to the practice of meditation. You may experience feelings of resentment, frustration, or anxiety. Simply acknowledge the feelings. Stay with them. It is a way of discovering yourself.

As you watch your mind drift, as you become anxious, as you get frustrated – recognize that you are getting to know your true self.

- Consider yourself with kindness and love.

You will slowly understand how your mind works. Always assume an attitude of loving acceptance.

Chapter 8: How to Sustain Your Meditation Practice

There are several things you can do to help you sustain your meditation practice.

- Meditate every day.

It does not have to be for a long period of time. The important thing is to do the practice on a regular basis. Invest on this quiet time for yourself. Consider it as a precious gift to yourself.

- Whenever you find the opportunity, take the time to pause.

Take a few seconds or minutes from your daily routine and focus on your breath. Get in touch with your body. Feel the life going through it. This will increase your self-awareness and will enable you to establish contact with your true self.

- Take the time to appreciate the fact that you are seeking spiritual awakening.

Make time to read up on Buddhist teachings to deepen your appreciation of the practice of meditation. Find out more about the Four Noble Truths, as well as the Noble Eight-fold Path. You can find many resources to help deepen your knowledge – CD's, books, and inspirational footages you can access through the web.

- Do not be too hard on yourself.

If you miss a day or two of meditation, simply pick up where you left off and resume the practice without guilt or discomfort.

- Do not evaluate your practice.

Do what you can, accepting what unfolds. Trust your innate capacity to enrich your life.

- Seek help.

If you feel the need for guidance, do not hesitate to seek the assistance of a mentor or a person experienced in the practice of meditation.

- Go on a retreat.

It can be for a few hours, an entire day, a whole weekend, or even longer. A retreat can help deepen and nourish your practice.

Conclusion

Thank you again for purchasing this book!

I hope this book was able to help you realize that you can practice meditation even when you have a busy lifestyle. You can do meditation in many simple, practical and convenient ways.

The next step is to apply the suggested short proactive meditations – even when you are on the go, and enjoy the full benefits of effective meditation.

Finally, if you enjoyed this book, then I'd like to ask you for a favor, would you be kind enough to leave a review for this book on Amazon? I would appreciate it very much!

Visit Amazon to leave a review: https://www.amazon.com/dp/B01MXPKMWJ

Thank you and good luck!

Here is a preview of my other book *"Mindfulness: A Mindful Eternity in Meditation – Mindfulness Meditation Guide for All and All Moments"*

...According to ancient texts, "mindfulness" is derived from the word, *sati*, a Pali term, which refers to attention, remembering, and awareness. Pali has been the language for interpreting and teaching the lessons of the Buddha. It is said that in 1921, *sati* was translated into "mindfulness" to better understand its concept. At the same time, the meaning of "mindfulness" has also been modified for psychotherapy application. Today, it now includes a wide range of concepts as well as practices.

Aspects of Mindfulness

While awareness is inexplicitly powerful, attention is more powerful given that it denotes focused awareness. When you are aware of what transpires within and around you, you will be able to start to disengage yourself from difficult emotion and mental preoccupation. In some instances, disengaging from suffering or a demanding situation is quite simple. Take the case of a mentally retarded individual. Just because he is developmentally challenged does not mean he cannot manage his anger. A mentally retarded individual may simply shift his attention to the palms of his hands once he notices he is angry. Consequently, instead of suppressing or controlling intense emotions, human beings can redirect their attention in order to manage how they feel.

"Remembering" is another aspect of mindfulness. The term "remembering" does not refer to recalling the past. "Remembering" entails being aware and paying attention, focusing on the significance of intention in practicing mindfulness. Simply put, this aspect entails reminding oneself "to remember to become aware" in every moment or situation.

On the other hand, "mindfulness" is more than just being aware for the sake of being so. According to Buddhist scholars, *attention, remembering (sati)*, and *awareness* are all present, say, when a thief takes aim at his victim with malevolence in his heart. This is not the goal of Buddhist psychology or what psychotherapists try to foster. The purpose of mindfulness based on its ancient or original discourse is to discard unnecessary suffering through nourishing insight into the material world's nature and the workings of the mind. Practicing mindfulness involves working with the states of mind for the purpose of abiding peacefully in whatever circumstance one is in.

Individuals are able to manage their minds, developing the ability to become "street smart" through mindfulness. It aids in recognizing when to cultivate mental qualities, including concentration, effort, alertness, kindness, and loving in order to alleviate suffering in a skillful manner. For instance, if you feel lazy, you may try to increase your energy level either in your mind or body or if you are self-critical during meditation, you may incorporate a little compassion.

It should be noted that mindfulness is not a stand-alone formula to alleviate or discard suffering. Mindfulness alone is insufficient for achieving happiness. However, it establishes a solid groundwork for various factors. Rather than addressing mindfulness as a goal in itself, the classical literature usually discussed it based on its function. It is a significant part of a project, which is intended to displace habits of the mind that are entrenched and cause unhappiness, including unpleasant emotions of greed, anger, or envy, or behaviors that cause harm to oneself and others.

Meanwhile, in psychotherapy, the recent focus on mindfulness is a strategic rectification to some modern trends in treatment. More often than not, therapists, even those with the purest intentions, are inclined to "correct" the problems of the patients while unknowingly bypassing self-understanding and self-acceptance.

In the next chapters, it will be demonstrated that human behavioral and emotional problems are factors that can be magnified through one's instinctive efforts to alleviate discomfort by impelling into activities that seek change. The modern approach of a mindfulness-oriented agenda is first and foremost, awareness and acceptance, followed by change…

Go to Amazon to check out the rest of *"Mindfulness: A Mindful Eternity in Meditation"*: https://www.amazon.com/dp/B01N10WSXQ

Made in the USA
Middletown, DE
13 September 2017